animals.

Blue whales swim **looooooong** distances across the ocean.

Imagine if a blue whale came to stay.

What would she do?

What if a blue whale went on holiday?

She would be **too big** to fit in the aeroplane!

Blue whales grow to 33 metres long. That's about the length of an aeroplane!

Blue whales are also very heavy. They weigh the same as

40 elephants.

Several jumbo jets might just be able to carry the weight of one whale.

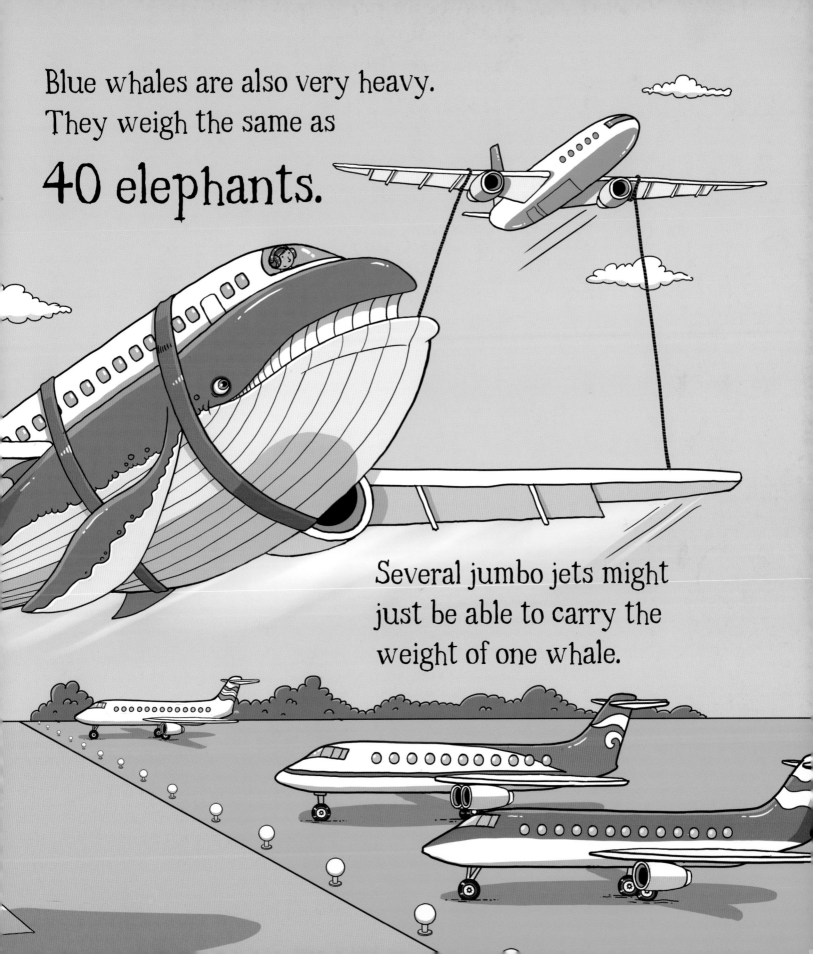

Could a whale swim to the Moon?

During its long life, a blue whale can swim about one million kilometres.

That's like swimming around the world

25 times.

It's further than going to the

Moon and back!

Would a blue whale baby grow as fast as me?

When blue whales are born they weigh 3 tonnes. As a baby they are already one of the **biggest animals** on the planet!

A baby whale can grow
3 centimetres and put on

90 kilograms

in just one day.

That's as much
as a grown-up
man weighs!

What if a blue whale was hungry?

A blue whale can eat

4 tonnes

of shrimp-like animals called krill every day.

That's the same as 20,000 sausages!

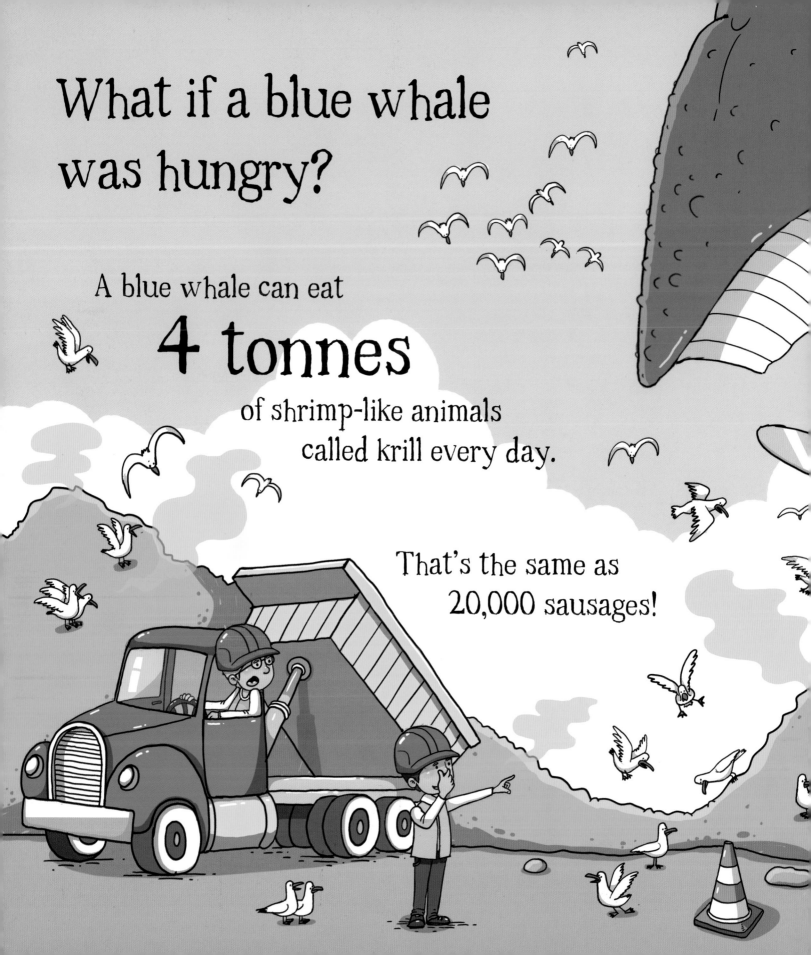

Each krill is just the size of a **jellybean!**

What if a blue whale tried synchronised swimming?

She would be a natural! Blue whales make lots of movements at the water's surface.

They **slap** the water with their fins... make a splash

with their tails... and they can **leap** out of the water. But they **don't** look so good in a swimming cap!

Would a whale be a good friend?

She would give...

...ENORMOUS

hugs and lots of love.

A blue whale is a gentle giant with the biggest heart in the animal world. It's the size of a small car!

What if a whale threw a party?

She could fill the room with **balloons.**

Whales breathe in and out through blowholes in their head. One blue whale breath would be enough to blow up...

250 balloons!

What if a blue whale stayed the night?

She wouldn't need a toothbrush. Her mouth may be massive, but she has

no teeth

at all – not even tiny ones!

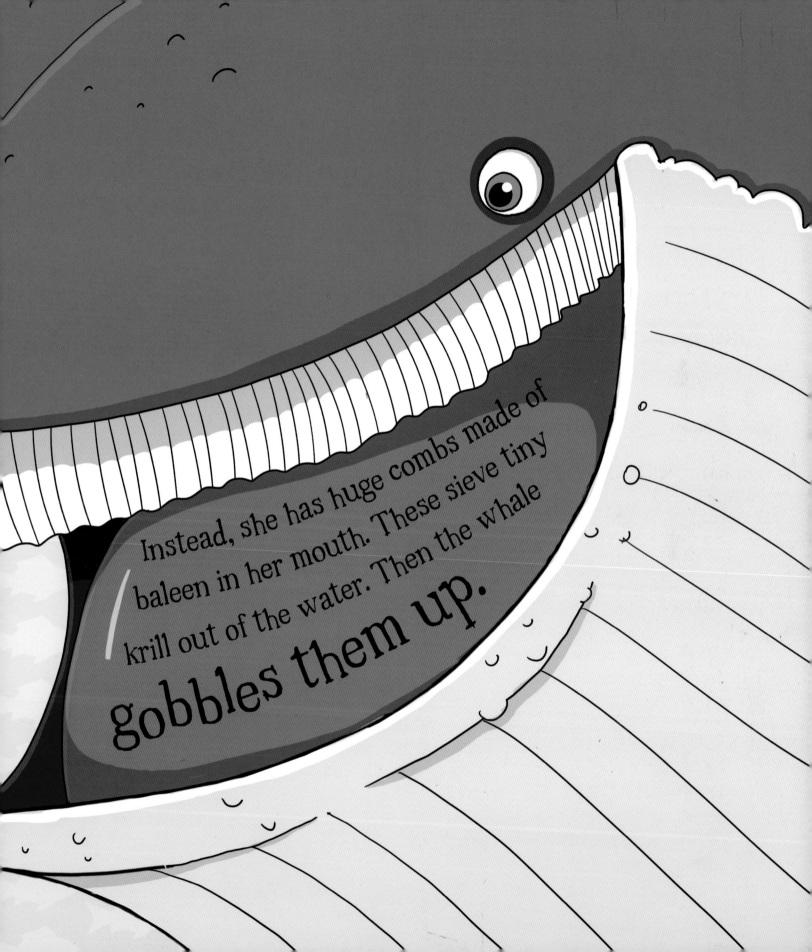

Instead, she has huge combs made of baleen in her mouth. These sieve tiny krill out of the water. Then the whale gobbles them up.

Blue whales **love** to sing.

However, their voices are so deep that we humans **can't hear them!**

Their songs can be heard by other whales far across the ocean. That makes a blue whale the **loudest** animal on the planet.

More about blue whales

Blue whale is pointing to the places where she lives.
Can you see where you live?

FACT FILE

There are 85 types of whale, and the blue whale is the biggest of them all.

Some whales, like the blue whale, only feed on tiny animals, but most of them are hunters that eat seals, fish and squid.

A blue whale can't swallow anything bigger than a beach ball.

Whales sometimes live together in groups called pods.

A blue whale's tongue is about 4 metres long and weighs as much as an Asian elephant.

Areas where blue whales live

NORTH AMERICA

PACIFIC OCEAN

SOUT AMER

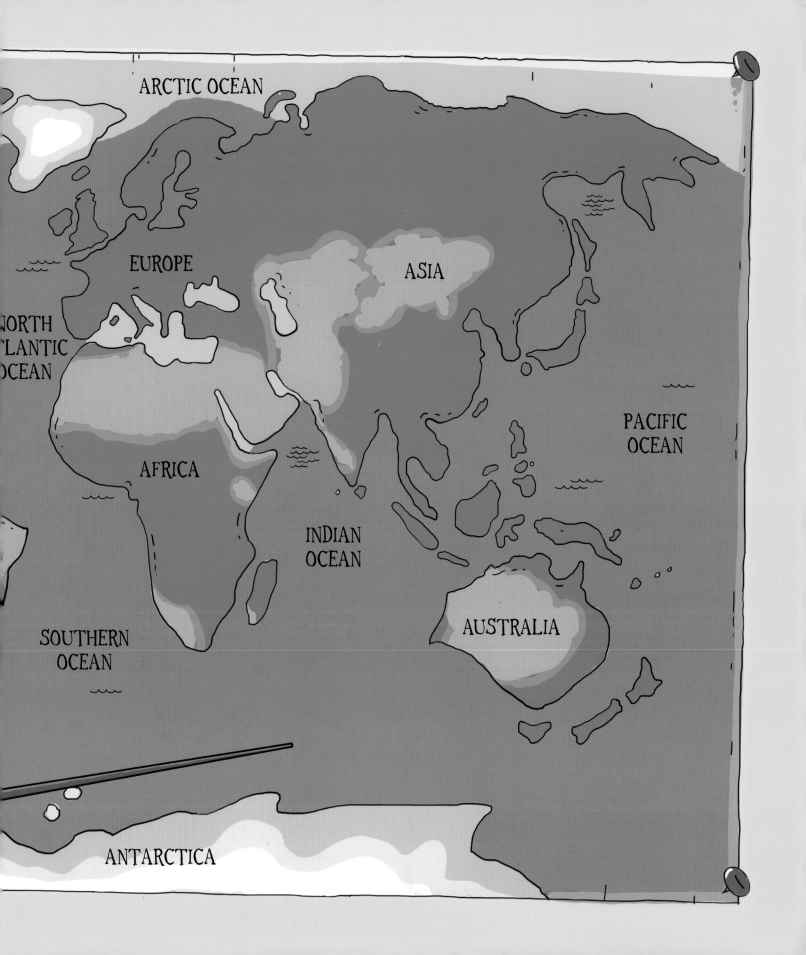

Greetings from the ocean!

POST CARD

It was a great holiday, but I'm glad to be back in the sea. I've been swimming across the ocean, gulping down krill. I can hear my friends calling (they are about 1000 kilometres away, but I've got fabulous hearing!) so I'm going to tell them all about my trip.

Love,
Blue Whale X

SENT BY BLUE WHALE POST
SOUTHERN OCEAN

The Pryce Family
221 High Street
Exeter
EX6 9ED
UK

5148263560809178379